Worship

Restoration Movement

by
James Steven
Assistant Curate, Welling Parish Church, Kent

GROVE BOOKS LIMITED
Bramcote   Nottingham   NG9 3DS

CONTENTS

ACKNOWLEDGMENTS

I gladly acknowledge the help and guidance of Phil Rogers, Pastor of New Life Christian Church in Lee, who not only spent a profitable afternoon with the Group for the Renewal of Worship but who has also enabled me to understand many different aspects of Restorationist worship. Also thanks to Margaret Robinson for typing the manuscript, to colleagues and friends in the parish of St. John's for their patience, to members of G.R.O.W. for their encouragement, and to my wife Rachel for being my most enthusiastic supporter.

THE COVER PICTURE

is by Peter Ashton

First Impression October 1989

ISSN 0144-1728
ISBN 1 85174 125 9

1. INTRODUCTION

The Background

Since its beginning in the 1960s the Restoration Movement (also known by outsiders as the 'house church movement') has grown and developed into a national phenomenon, and is now a well established feature of British church life. Documentation of the Movement's growth has been more than adequately handled by Dr. Andrew Walker, a Russian Orthodox, in his book *Restoring the Kingdom*.[1] The Movement was originally part of the Charismatic Movement in the 1960s, and then in the early 1970s it began to take on its distinctive characteristics, as the Charismatic Movement diverged into two main streams, Renewal and Restorationism.

The fundamental difference between these two streams was the way in which they responded to the Spirit. Those in Renewal, focussed in the 1970s on the Fountain Trust, sought to live out the implications of charismatic life within already established church institutions. The majority of these people belonged to Catholic, Anglican or Methodist churches. Restorationism, however, sought to go further in radically altering church structures according to their perception of Biblical principles. They sensed that the new wine could not be contained within the old wineskins and so the old structures had to go. It is important to point out that the great majority of Restoration churches have their roots in the independent, Free Church tradition (e.g. Brethren, Independent Baptists, Evangelical Free Churches, Assemblies of God), and they were therefore used to the concept of local autonomy. This made structure changes comparatively easy since, unlike Anglicans, Catholics and Methodists, they were unlikely to meet with an 'ecclesiastical ceiling' to their reorganization and change.

In the early 1970s the many small house church fellowships began to order themselves in larger fellowship networks. There was talk of 'restoring the Kingdom', which meant the ordering of church life along Biblical principles. Various Bible weeks provided foci for the Movement (e.g. Capel Bible Week, and later, Downs and Dales Bible Weeks). One can discern different strands within the Movement as it continues today. Two examples are the Harvestime Fellowship, led by Bryn Jones in Bradford, and New Frontiers (formerly Coastlands) led by Terry Virgo in the South of England. Another strand to the Movement would be Gerald Coates' Pioneer Trust based in Surrey. It is debatable whether one ought to include the Ichthus Fellowship in South London, within Restorationist categories.[2] Roger Forster, the leader of the fellowship, would not recognize Ichthus as being Restorationist. Dissimilarities would include the fact that Ichthus is more open to working with other denominations, and the fact that it has a much broader definition of women's ministry. There are, however, significant similarities in that Ichthus is independent and autonomous and shares the worship style of Restorationism.[3]

[1] Hodder and Stoughton. First printed 1985. 2nd. edition 1988, 3rd edition, 1989.
[2] For reasons such as these Andrew Walker regards Ichthus as lying outside his categories of Restorationism. See *Restoring the Kingdom* (1988), p.37.
[3] Andrew Walker describes Ichthus as Open Brethren and Renewal Pentecostalist in ethos. (*Op. cit.*, p.37.)

3

Why a Grove Booklet?

There are a number of reasons why a fresh appraisal of Restorationism in terms of its worship may be productive.

1. In the first instance, worship is at the heart of the Movement's life. This has been true both of Restorationism and Renewal since one of the consequences of the rediscovery of the Holy Spirit has been an emphasis on the importance of worship. Andrew Walker, in describing the kind of life you would lead if you were a Restorationist, writes: 'You will spend a great deal of time in worship whilst you are in the Kingdom.'[1]

2. Secondly, it is important to recognize the growing influence of the Movement on the wider church's worship. Individual song and hymn writers such as Graham Kendrick[2] (Ichthus Fellowship, London) and Dave Fellingham (Clarendon Church, Hove) have written material which is being widely used across denominations. Within the Anglican church this is particularly true of those churches of an evangelical, charismatic flavour. The publication of *Songs of Fellowship* by Kingsway has put a large selection of Restoration songs in the hands and on the lips of many Christian worshippers. The annual gathering of Spring Harvest introduces many people of all denominations to this music.[3]

3. Thirdly, it appears that there has been little evaluation of the forms and theology of worship in the Restoration Movement from an outsider's perspective. Walker's work concentrates on matters concerning church order and discipline: apostleship, church shepherding, and the relationship of the different fellowships to each other. Although he gives descriptions of their worship, his purpose was not to assess its implications for the wider church. A recent Anglican response to the challenge of Restorationism by Tony Higton and Gilbert Kirby[4] touches upon worship but does not go into detail.[5] If the Movement is here to stay then those outside it need, at the very least, to listen to what is going on in its worship life.

The Aim of the Booklet

The aim of this booklet is to make a description and an appraisal of worship in the Restoration Movement. The description concentrates on the forms and theology of worship found in the New Frontiers network, although other fellowships have influenced the study (e.g. New Life Christian Fellowship in Lincoln in connection with music). The appraisal is from an evangelical Anglican perspective. The booklet will attempt to make an evaluation of Restorationist worship which does justice to the insights and challenges it presents to the wider church, does not ignore the further questions that an Anglican would need to ask about it.

[1] *Restoring the Kingdom*, pp.197-198.
[2] Graham Kendrick would not regard himself as being a Restorationist, but I include him because he shares in the Restorationist worship culture.
[3] It will be noted that I do not deal with the phenomenon of Make Way Praise Marches in this booklet. Although they could be said to be Restorationist in style, they draw together Christians of many different denominations and therefore are not unique to Restorationism.
[4] *The Challenge of the Housechurches*, (Latimer Study No. 27).
[5] *op. cit.* pp.30-32.

4

2. FORMS OF RESTORATION WORSHIP

1. Celebration, Congregation, Cell
A common feature of Restorationism is its three-tier structure to worship life. Three levels of meeting have been developed[1] which are designed to meet the differing needs of the worshipper.[1]

. . . Celebration
This is the largest of the three gatherings and would bring together a large fellowship (over 200), or a number of fellowships in a locality. The worship at a Bible Week would also come into this category. This kind of meeting is usually led by a worship leader and musicians on a platform at the front. They would have prepared a framework for the meeting, which would tend to flow from more jubilant praise into more contemplative songs; worship is seen as a journey into the presence of God. Individual contributions from the congregation will probably be limited to a selected few. There would be Bible teaching as well.

. . . Congregation
The congregational meeting envisages about 50-200 people. This would be ideal for a small fellowship or a number of housegroups meeting together. A large church is often split up into congregational units. Each person is free to participate spontaneously, although the worship leader has the responsibility to keep the meeting on course. The musicians will not so much set the musical agenda but rather respond to congregational input. The controlling model of this type of meeting is the body fellowship model of 1 Corinthians 14.26.

. . . Cell
These are the housegroup meetings, and their aim is to provide care and support for members. Worship usually takes the form of singing, either led by a guitarist or unaccompanied. There would also be time for Bible study, sharing experiences and needs, intercession and social enjoyment. The atmosphere is more intimate than the bigger celebration or congregation meetings and therefore lends itself to building the confidence of each member to contribute.

2. Sunday Worship
What might it be like to worship with a Restoration church on a Sunday? The following description is an attempt to give an impression of such an event. The account is generalized and so no doubt it will differ in details from some fellowships. It is hoped however that it will be close to a typical Sunday congregation style gathering.

On arrival at the meeting place (which may for example be a cinema, a hired hall, or a disused warehouse), you are greeted as you enter. You will probably be given a news sheet and a song book (either *Songs of Fellowship* or *Power Praise*), although you may not be given anything at all (a most disorientating experience for an Anglican), as some churches

[1] See Graham Kendrick (ed.), *Ten Worshipping Churches*, (MARC Europe, 1987), pp.90-93, 167-170.

rely entirely on the overhead projector to provide the words of the songs. However, you will never receive a printed service order - there are none! As you then try to find a seat (moveable plastic chairs, not pews) you are aware of the noise and activity around you. There is a great deal of greeting and chatting, and a sense of enjoyment in each other's company pervades.

The centre-piece for the gathering is a platform[1] at the front. Here the musicians and singers sit with or near the leaders. The chairs will probably form an arc around the platform at the front, so as to enhance participation by the worshippers. The sound will be controlled by a mixing desk at the back.

The first phase of the meeting will be dominated by songs and hymns, and will last anything between 15-45 minutes. The congregation participate in many ways. Individuals may start a song, or read a passage from Scripture (often without identifying where it has come from). During the singing people may dance, raise their hands in the air, clap, kneel or lie prostrate. Sometimes a song may be followed by a 'clap offering', when everyone applauds in thanksgiving to God. You may witness what is called 'singing in the Spirit' or 'singing in tongues', where the whole congregation will strike off into wordless musical notes and rhythms, not in tune with each other but in marvellous unity-in-diversity with each other. Musicians can both introduce and reinforce this practice.

Notices will probably follow this first phase, and then an offering. Children leave the main meeting to go to their own lessons. As they leave, the musicians may start a song or teach a new one, and this can lead to another phase of sung worship with contributions from the congregation, and this in turn leads to the preaching.

The sermon will follow on from a reading of Scripture and on average will last for about 45 minutes (not less than 20 minutes, and maybe up to an hour). The congregation are often eager to listen and are unlikely to complain about the length of the sermon. An opportunity for responding to the sermon is frequently given. This might be in the form of music and song developing the theme of the sermon. Prayer will be another response: individuals who want prayer will either be asked to stand up or asked to come to the front. It is assumed that worship will be a transforming experience for the participants.

The meeting will then be given an ending by the leadership, but there is little sense of people hurrying to leave. Prayer will continue in small groups, and others will stay to chat together.

Having slipped away from the scene you will begin to reflect on the worship and how it compares with your own style of service. If you are an Anglican you will be aware of certain events which you have missed.

---

[1] 'Platform' is used here to define the area used by leaders and musicians, which may or may not be raised above floor level.

... Confession

There was no official provision for corporate confession, although if you went regularly you would find that occasionally confession happens spontaneously, led by the leadership or a member of the congregation. This would nearly always be in response to the sermon. Very rarely would any confession occur in the early part of the meeting.

... Bible Reading

People bring Bibles and may read passages at the front or from the congregation. Recognizing the set reading for the day is not always easy, although the reading before the sermon is closest to it in function. Often a church will be following a theme of readings which the leadership will have decided.

... Creed

There is no creed whereby the congregation regularly state what they believe. Declarations, often taking the form of Biblical statements, are the nearest equivalent: individuals declare Biblical truths about God and his Church, usually in the singing phase of the meeting. Some of the songs function in a similar fashion, a good recent example being Graham Kendrick's 'We believe in God the Father'.[1]

... Holy Communion

The practice of Breaking of Bread, as most Restorationists prefer to call it (revealing their Free Church roots), varies from congregation to congregation. On average it will occur about once a month. The common practice is for the institution narrative from 1 Corinthians 11 to be read, followed by administration, which will vary according to what is wanting to be emphasized. For example, everyone may wait so as to consume the bread and wine in one action together, emphasizing the unity which Christ's death brings. Alternatively, bread and wine are consumed individually, either in one's seat or perhaps after having gone to the front to receive, emphasizing the importance of feeding individually on Christ.

3. Hymnody

One of the main characteristics of the widespread charismatic awakening over the past twenty years has been the increase in worship songs. The Restoration Movement has shared in this phenomenon and its present use of hymnody has the following characteristics:

(a) Many of the songs are based on Bible texts. Verses from Psalms are often used, but other parts of the Bible are used as well. David Fellingham, for example, has written a number of songs from Ephesians. Such songs are ususally one or two verse songs, maybe with accompanying chorus.

(b) The style of song usually falls into one of three main categories. First, the lively fast tempo songs which often express the joy of being a

[1] *Make Way Handbook* (Kingsway, 1988), p.108.

Christian (e.g. 'I am a new creation', (SHF 179), 'Come on and celebrate' (SHF 69)). Secondly, the slower tempo songs which express intimacy and closeness between God and the worshipper (e.g. 'I love you Lord, and I lift my voice' (SHF 203), 'When I look into your holiness' (SHF 601)). Thirdly, the mid-tempo songs which emphasize the majesty of God. Such songs draw, upon the divine Kingship themes in the Psalms and the imagery of the Lamb reigning with the Father in the Book of Revelation (e.g. 'God of glory, we exalt your name' (SHF 136), 'For thou O Lord art high above all the earth' (SHF 112), 'At your feet we fall, mighty risen Lord' (SHF 25)). This third category has been a recent emphasis of Restorationism.

(c) Songs which come into the category of hymns (i.e. three or more verses) are also sung. Some of these are traditional hymns, and some more contemporary. Graham Kendrick's work is the most obvious example of the latter. 'Meekness and Majesty' (2) and 'The Servant King' (SHF 120) are fine contemporary hymns on the theme of the incarnation.

(d) Restoration churches tend to be flexible in the way that they use songs and hymns. The single-verse songs usually focus on one Scriptural truth and are often sung more than once in order to enhance meditation upon that truth. Traditional hymns are often sung in a non-traditional manner. For example, a hymn could be repeated on a number of Sundays running, but with only a selected number of verses being sung.

---

[1] *Songs and Hymns of Fellowship* (Songs of Fellowship Books 1, 2 & 3, and Kingsway, 1988 Hymns of Fellowship). All S.H.F. numbers quoted in the booklet are from this edition.
[2] *Make Way Handbook*, p.113, No. 9.

3. THEOLOGY OF RESTORATION WORSHIP

Theological Background

In order to appreciate the Restorationists' understanding of worship it is important to have an overview of their theological framework. Despite some differences in emphasis between churches, it is possible to discern a common core of theological understanding.[1]

1. Underlying all the Restorationist priorities is an exclusive adherence to the Bible. Restorationism is Conservative Evangelicalism at its most radical. By 'radical' Restorationists mean a return to the origins, roots[2] or sources of pure Christianity. They therefore go behind Christian tradition in order to get at the pure tradition of the Bible. The consequence of this returning to the roots is a constant re-appraisal of every aspect of church life and structure in the light of Scriptural principles. 'Constant change is here to stay!' was one of the early catch-phrases of Restorationism.

2. Another distinct emphasis within the Movement is its theology of the Holy Spirit which most closely resembles Pentecostalism. The 'baptism in the Holy Spirit' is seen as essential for each Christian if they are to have power for witness, effectiveness in prayer and entrance into the realm of spiritual gifts. Unlike the Pentecostal 'second blessing' theology, Restorationists consider baptism in the Holy Spirit as part of Christian initiation. Repentance and faith are therefore not sufficient for authentic Christian life. They have to be accompanied by baptism in the Holy Spirit for complete initiation to have occurred.[3] Normally baptism in the Spirit would be authenticated by speaking in tongues. Church life is also structured charismatically, in other words, according to the gifts of Spirit. For example, elders are appointed on the basis that there is a recognized 'anointing' by the Spirit of a person's gift for eldership. When they are appointed, the apostle in oversight will lay hands on the elder as an outward acknowledgement of what God himself has done by his Spirit.

3. Characteristic of the structure of leadership is the re-emergence of the New Testament office of apostle (Ephesians 4.11f has been important in this connection). The main functions of apostles are seen to be church planting (or foundation laying along the lines of 1 Corinthians 3.10) and overall oversight of churches. It is to them that the elders are to be accountable.[1] The principle of accountability is an important element in the structure of Restorationism. Each Christian must submit himself or herself to an overseer's authority (whether a housegroup leader, local church elder, or apostle) in order to grow as a disciple. This ensures that everyone is open to correction and that one's whole lifestyle (time, possessions, family etc.) is orientated to God's priorities.

[1] For an example of the New Frontiers' perspective see Terry Virgo, *Restoration in the Church*, (Kingsway, 1985).
[2] Arthur Wallis, a very important leading figure in early Restorationism, points out in his book *The Radical Christian* that the word 'radical' has its origins in the Latin *radix*, or root.
[3] See *Learning to Worship*, Phil Rogers (Word, 1988), pp.33-37 for a Restorationist argument for this point.
[4] See Higton and Kirby *The Challenge of the Housechurches*, (Latimer Study No.27) pp.16-20 for further details.

4. Andrew Walker calls the Restorationists a 'Kingdom people'. Many songs which are sung (as mentioned above) emphasize the sovereignty and majesty of God, and the ascended Christ seated at the Father's right hand. This is matched by a corresponding sense of being Kingdom people, the soldiers of the King. Being a Restorationist Christian means a thorough commitment to God's purposes of restoring the Kingdom (i.e. restoring pure Biblical Christianity), whether it be evangelism, worship, or submitting to oversight in the local church. Andrew Walker writes: 'For them the only Church worth belonging to is the Church militant. They often like to see themselves as a battleship ready for war; denominations are viewed as luxury cruisers'.[1]

Theology of Worship

For the Restorationist, one of the major consequences of the Kingdom being restored is a renewal of worship. 'Renewed worship is an integral part of what God is doing today in bringing the Church back to how God intended it to be: worship is an essential part of God's restoration programme.'[2] The implication of this is that the Church has neglected true worship. Some of the suggested reasons for this are liberal theology, a lack of the Holy Spirit, services structured so as to leave no time for worship (e.g. a long sermon instead), cultural embarrassment (e.g. raising arms not the done thing), and church members who have no living, personal relationship with God. This neglect of true worship is characteristic not only of the liberal wing of the Church, but also of evangelicals. Reference is often made to A. W. Tozer's phrase, coined in the early 1960s, that worship is the 'missing jewel of the Evangelical Church'.[3] Phil Rogers sees this as 'a perceptive but devastating description of Bible-believing churches of these days'.[4]

It is since the Charismatic Movement that this missing jewel is seen by the Restorationist to have been rediscovered. The Spirit has brought a fresh appreciation of the importance of worship. New forms are characterized by a freedom of expression and spontaneity which has led the Restorationists, and also those in Renewal, to move away from their traditional worship structures in an attempt to explore this new found freedom. In the wake of this rediscovery there has been a fresh impetus to reflect theologically about worship. The following is an outline of their thinking on restored worship.

1. God is seeking worshippers—John 4.19-24[5]

In the words of the Westminster Longer Catechism (1647), quoted both by Phil Rogers[6] and Dave Fellingham,[7] 'Man's chief end is to glorify God

---

[1] *Restoring the Kingdom* (1988), p.144.
[2] D. Fellingham, *Worship Restored,* p.84.
[3] After his book: *Worship: The Missing Jewel* (Christian Publications, 1961).
[4] *Learning to Worship,* p.28.
[5] I do not quote Graham Kendrick in the following discussion, but he also has written on the importance of this text. See his *Worship* (Kingsway, 1984), chapters 6-8. The text seems to be a seminal one for those writing on worship from a charismatic perspective.
[6] *Learning to Worship,* p.14.
[7] *Worship Restored,* p.74.

and fully enjoy him forever'. Men and women are created for worship. The basis for understanding the nature of this worship is found in the conversation between Jesus and the Samaritan woman. First, God is seeking worshippers (v.23). He is primarily concerned with the heart of each individual worshipper. 'God is after people who are totally given over to him—fully committed, utterly devoted—who love him, adore him and serve him with every fibre of their being.'[1] This means that worship cannot be limited to a meeting on Sunday but is a whole lifestyle. It also means that modes of expression in worship are of secondary importance. Phil Rogers infers from Jesus and the woman's discussion of the place of worship (Jn. 4.19-22) that one of the important principles of true worship is that it is 'to do with the kind of people we are rather than the kind of services we attend'.[2]

Secondly, the kind of worshippers for whom God seeks are those who worship in Spirit and in truth (v.23). 'Worship is a spiritual exercise and can only be carried out in the Spirit'.[3] It is axiomatic for true worshippers that they be baptized in the Holy Spirit. They must also worship 'in truth', which has a double application. First the content of worship such as songs must be controlled by Scripture (as Colossians 3.16-17 makes clear), and secondly the expression of worship must be true to an individual's experience of God. 'Worship must be a meaningful expression of the truth of God that is real to me in my own life'.[4]

2. Models for Worship Meetings

When worshippers gather together to worship corporately there is an expectation that 'God will be in the midst', a phrase much used in Restoration circles. There also has also developed an expectation that each meeting will also have a clearly defined purpose. This has arisen in reaction to the rather chaotic nature of meetings early on in the Movement's life, where it was felt that there were too many aspects to a single gathering. The cell-congregation-celebration structure has been the practical outworking of this 'meeting to purpose' (another Restorationist phrase). Within this three-fold structure, different Scriptural models will operate, depending upon their suitability to the purpose of the meeting. The following are the models used:[5]

(a) The Body (1 Corinthians 12-14; Romans 12.3-8)

The emphasis of the Body model is upon every-member participation under the guidance and inspiration of the Holy Spirit. Such a model has been commonplace not only among Restoration fellowships but also amongst churches involved in Renewal. The gifts or manifestations of the Spirit are given to members of the church for their mutual upbuilding. It is the congregational style meeting that functions on this model.

[1] *Learning to Worship*, p.18.
[2] *Learning to Worship*, p.17.
[3] *Learning to Worship*, p.17.
[4] *Learning to Worship*, p.17.
[5] See *Learning to Worship*, p.74-78.

(b) The Synagogue (Luke 4.16f; Acts 13.14; 1 Timothy 4.13)
This model is based on the reading of and instruction in the Law given by the Rabbis. The reading and teaching of the Scriptures could be part of any level of meeting.

(c) The Love Feast (e.g. Acts 2.44-46; 1 Corinthians 11.17-34)
The sharing of bread and wine is seen as an important way of feeding upon the Lord and renewing the bonds of fellowship. Like the Synagogue model, this could be part of any meeting.

(d) The Prayer Meeting (e.g. Acts 3.23-31)
Intercession could be part of any meeting.

(e) Proclamation (e.g. Luke 10.1-16; Acts 2.14ff)
This model is different from the Synagogue model in that this envisages evangelistic preaching.

(f) The Tabernacle of David (Acts 15.16-18; 1 Chronicles 16; Psalms; Revelation 4-5)
The emphasis of this model is the extravagant giving of praise seen as characteristic of the Chronicler's account of David's entry into Jerusalem with the Ark, and its subsequent period in Jerusalem. It is seen as particularly suitable for a celebration meeting. The underlying principle is the 'priestly' duty of the worshipper to bring a sacrifice of praise and thanksgiving to God, and it thus describes a 'from us to God' movement. Because this model is the most distinctive to Restorationism it deserves fuller analysis.

3. The Tabernacle of David
To most Christians the books of Chronicles might seem a strange place to receive inspiration for the worshipping life of the church. 1 Chronicles 1-9 for example most closely resembles the solemn reading of church notices (and that is probably being generous!), hardly a blueprint for worship 'in the Spirit'. However, as 1 Chronicles begins to gather pace in subsequent chapters, the reader will stumble across one of the Chronicler's chief concerns, the establishing of the worship life of the Temple under David and Solomon. It is the Davidic period (1 Chronicles 11-29) that has become the source for the 'Tabernacle of David' model. When Restorationists use the phrase 'Tabernacle of David', they are referring primarily to the order of worship that David inaugurated when he brought the Ark into Jerusalem (the fact that David pitched a tent for the Ark (1 Chronicles 15.1) is not relevant to the use of the term). When used as a model, it refers to the principles of worship that can be learnt from this period in Israel's life.

The significance of this model is demonstrated by recent Restorationist writing. Graham Kendrick in his editorial introduction to *Ten Worshipping Churches*[1], comments on new forms of worship. He says, 'It is interesting that a number of churches mention the period in the Old Testament after David brought the Ark of God to Jerusalem as a useful "model" for the

[1] G. Kendrick (ed.) *Ten Worshipping Churches*, (MARC Europe, 1987).

organization and practice of worship in the Church'. He is referring to three of the ten churches in the book, all of whom seem to be of the Restorationist mould. New Life Christian Fellowship in Lincoln (ch.5)[1], Poplars Christian Fellowship in Worksop (ch.7)[2] and Clarendon Church in Brighton and Hove (ch.9).[3] In general it appears that those who write most about the Tabernacle of David model are the worship leaders within the Movement. Two examples are David Fellingham at Clarendon Church in Brighton and Hove, and Chris Bowater at the New Life Christian Fellowship in Lincoln. The latter confesses that 'a favourite theme of mine is the restoration of the Tabernacle of David'.[4]

The model is both descriptive and prescriptive. It is descriptive in that Restorationists have found the Davidic worship in Chronicles to be a reflection of the kind of worship they have developed, particularly in the celebration style. But it also functions prescriptively in that the narrative in Chronicles provides important principles for establishing the nature of true worship. A verse which is often quoted to legitimize the use of the Tabernacle of David model for the Christian Church is Acts 15.16. The Apostle James' phrase 'David's fallen tent' (New International Version), translated by the New American Standard Version as 'the Tabernacle of David which has fallen', is by some assumed to be a direct reference to the era of worship under David.[5] However, this is more a case of reading the meaning of a Restorationist term into the text, rather than letting the text speak for itself.[6] A more appropriate verse would be 2 Timothy 3.16. The following are some examples of how the Davidic narrative has been used to provide principles:

(i) The death of Uzzah—worship must be Biblical
1 Chronicles 13 describes the abortive attempt of David to bring the Ark into Jerusalem on an ox-cart. God's wrath broke out against Uzzah, and the reason given by David was because they had not obeyed God's instructions for moving the Ark (1 Chronicles 15.13). In the light of this it is important to ensure that patterns of worship, no matter how charismatic they are, have their foundations in Biblical truth.[7]

(ii) The Ark—God in the midst
One of the most significant features of the Ark of the Covenant for Israel was that it was a visible sign of the presence of God (e.g. Numbers 10.35, 1 Samuel 4.22, Psalm 132:8). Its installation in Jerusalem by David as a focus for worship establishes the important principle that the worship must be worship with 'God in the midst'.

---

[1] op.cit. p.94.
[2] op.cit. pp.129-131.
[3] op.cit. p.165ff.
[4] Chris Bowater, *Creative Worship*, (Marshall Pickering, 1986), p.59.
[5] The logic of David Fellingham's chapter 4 ('Prophetic Worship') in *Worship Restored* appears to follow this line of understanding.
[6] The traditional understanding of this text is that the Tabernacle of David is a general reference to the house of David (e.g. F. F. Bruce in *The Book of Acts* (Eerdmans, 1981), p.130). This verse therefore describes the establishing of the Messianic Kingdom and has no specific reference to worship.
[7] Chris Bowater, *Creative Worship*, (Marshall Pickering, 1986), p.59.

(iii) David—a model worshipper.

The narrative of 1 Chronicles describes David as wearing a linen ephod and dancing and celebrating as the Ark is successfully transferred to Jerusalem (1 Chronicles 15.27,29). This incident is an example of his priestly ministry and provides an important principle for Restorationist worship, namely that it is to be wholehearted offering of oneself in a sacrifice of praise. This principle is probably the most fundamental to the Tabernacle of David model.

David has always tended to be an important figure in Restorationist theology. Andrew Walker comments, 'David is a key figure in Restoration hermeneutics and typology'.[1] David Fellingham writes of David as the one who combined the three-fold ministry of prophet, priest and king, a ministry which was fulfilled in Jesus and then through him given to the Church.[2] He writes concerning David: 'Anointed as king, he also wore the linen ephod of the priest, and had remarkable prophetic insights into God's purpose for the future'.[3] The implication for worship is three-fold: it is to be priestly in that worshippers offer a spiritual sacrifice of praise; it is to be prophetic, proclaiming God's character and declaring his purposes; it is to be kingly, demonstrating the authority of Christ (Psalm 149.6-9 is often quoted in this connection).[4] Also significant for Restorationists is the principle of anointing. In the Old Testament all three ministries of prophet, priest and king were initiated by anointing (e.g. 1 Kings 19.16, Exodus 28.41, 2 Samuel 5.3), the implication being that worshippers have to be anointed by the Spirit (i.e. by being baptized in the Spirit) before they can enter into worship. (Philippians 3.3, which says that Christians worship by the Spirit of God, is often quoted.)[5]

(iv) The musical Levites—Principles for musicians[6]

In preparation for the worship life in the Temple, David established a musical ministry around the Ark in Jerusalem (Chronicles 16.4-6, 37). A good example of the way a Restorationist would draw principles from these musicians is given by Chris Bowater in his booklet *When Music Becomes Ministry.*[7] The section for musicians (significantly called 'Discovering the Potential of your Priesthood'[8]—the musical Levites are seen as a model for a priestly sacrifice of praise) draws upon the Chronicles' material (though by no means exclusively) for principles. For example, mucisians are to have a calling (Levites were chosen and set apart by David: 1 Chronicles 15.16, 16.4, 25.1). They are to be thoroughly committed to their ministry and available to serve the congregation at all times (the Levites ministered regularly: 1 Chronicles 16.6, 37). It is also important to have someone in

[1] *Restoring the Kingdom* (1988), p.156.
[2] *Worship Restored* (Kingsway, 1987), chapter 3.
[3] *op. cit.,* p.35.
[4] *op. cit.,* p.36, 37 and as applied to musicians, R. Sheldon (Ed.), *In Spirit and in Truth* (Hodder and Stoughton, 1989), pp.63-68.
[5] E.g. Terry Virgo *Restoration in the Church* (Kingsway, 1985), p.60.
[6] It is interesting to note that musicians are seen to have an important role in spiritual warfare: see *Ten Worshipping Churches,* pp.132-3 for an example which draws upon Joshua at Jericho and Jehoshaphat in 2 Chronicles 20.
[7] Published by New Life Christian Fellowship, Lincoln.
[8] See also *Creative Worship,* Part III where the same material is covered.

charge of the musicians (there were chief musicians in Jerusalem: Kenaniah (1 Chronicles 15.22), Asaph, Heman and Jeduthun (1 Chronicles 25.1-8)).

(v) The Psalms[1]

The Psalms have an important role to play in Restorationist worship. First, they provide a model for expressive worship. As well as many references to singing, there are references to the raising of hands (e.g. Ps. 134.2), clapping (e.g. Ps. 47.1, Ps. 98.8), dancing (e.g. Ps. 150.4), bowing (e.g. Ps. 95.6) and shouting (e.g. Ps. 100.1). These are seen not merely as descriptions of worship, but as injunctions for worship. Being a Restorationist worshipper means that you do these things and do not just sing about them.[2] Secondly, they suggest that there should be variety not only in bodily expression but also in musical expression. Psalm 150 is a good example of this, and in quoting verses 3-6 Dave Fellingham writes, 'Traditionally the organ and the piano have been the prominent instruments for congregational accompaniment, but the Bible encourages a much wider variety of musical instruments'.[3] Thirdly the phenomenon of 'Selahs' in the Psalms (these are interpreted to mean musical interludes) has encouraged pauses in worship where the musicians play, allowing the congregation to meditate on the words of a song or words of Scripture. This idea has been developed by David Fellingham in terms of music interpreting God's truth. For example he writes, Why couldn't a trumpet or a flute express the heart of God for the lost?'[4] This he calls 'prophetic playing'.

The above is an attempt to summarize the way in which principles are drawn from the Tabernacle of David period. It is important to emphasize that the 'model' is a fluid one, and different Restoration teachers would emphasize different aspects of the above summary. However, the controlling principle would be that of David's whole-hearted priestly sacrifice of praise. This is seen as fundamental to every revival of worship, whether it be in Old Testament times (for example, after Nehemiah's rebuilding of Jerusalem's walls; Nehemiah 12.43)[5], or in the New Testament Church (1 Corinthians 12-14; Colossians 3.16; Ephesians 5.18-19), or in subsequent revivals such as the Reformation, the eighteenth. Century revival under Whitefield and Wesley, and the recent Charismatic Movement.[6] Such worship is also seen to be exhibited in the Book of Revelation (Revelation 4-5).

3. Entering the Presence of God

A description of Restorationist worship would not be complete without reference to the essential experience of coming face to face with God in

---

[1] I include the Psalms under this section because Restorationists assume that most of the Psalms were written in the Tabernacle of David era.
[2] See D. Fellingham *Worship Restored*, (Kingsway, 1987), Ch. 6, 'Expressions of Praise and Worship'.
[3] *op. cit.,* p.94.
[4] R. Sheldon (Ed.), *In Spirit and Truth,* (Hodder and Stoughton, 1989), p.65.
[5] *Worship Restored,* p.73.
[6] See *Worship Restored*, Chapter 2, 'The History of Worship in the Church'.

worship. This has been written about by a variety of people both within and outside Restorationism. Phil Rogers of New Frontiers, in describing this experience, sees a linguistic distinction in the way that the words 'praise' and 'worship' are used in the Bible.[1] Praise he sees in Scripture as something we are exhorted to do, and it is to do with commending or boasting of God's goodness and expressing thankfulness to him. Worship, as well as meaning offering our whole lives to God, can also mean an act of adoration. It is in this latter sense that he describes worship as primarily a response from the heart to a revelation of God through the Holy Spirit; there is wonder and awe for the worshipper. He describes the progression from praise to worship as follows: 'In praise we declare the great truths about the Lord, who he is and what he has done. But as we confess these words the Spirit within breathes life into them, and so we begin to wonder in our hearts. This revelation takes us from praise into worship'.[2] He sees this progression as needing to happen again and again within a time of 'Praise and Worship' (i.e. the non-preaching or teaching part of a worship meeting).

Graham Kendrick writes about this face-to-face encounter using the tabernacle of Moses as a visual aid.[3] The journey of the worshipper or worshipping assembly begins with 'entering his gates with thanksgiving and his courts with praise' (Ps. 100.4), and ends in the Holy of Holies (the way having been made open by Christ's death) with reverence and awe. 'Having been "doing" in the courts of praise, here our "doing" turns to "being", our action turns to stillness'.[4]

A song which expresses this communion is 'Within the veil' (SHF 616):

'Within the veil I now would come,
Into the Holy Place to look upon Thy face.
I see such beauty there, no other can compare,
I worship Thee, my Lord, within the veil.

John Wimber from the Vineyard Fellowship in the U.S.A. (he is not a Restorationist!), well known through his 'signs and wonders' ministry, has recently written on worship for the C.M.A. (Christian Music Association) *Worship* magazine. In the article, entitled 'Intimacy with God', he writes of five basic phases through which leaders in the Vineyard Fellowship attempt to lead the congregation. First, there is the call to worship. Secondly, there is the engagement 'which is the electrifying dynamic of connection to God and to each other'. Thirdly, having been awakened to the presence of God, the worshippers express their love for him which may be through praise, confession of sin or meditation. Expression then moves to a fourth phase, when God visits his people. 'Expression then moves to a zenith, a climactic point, not unlike physical lovemaking (doesn't Solomon use the same analogy in the Song of Songs?)'. This fourth phase may result in healings, conversions or deliverances. The fifth and final phase is the response of the congregation in the offering of themselves to God.

[1] See *Learning to Worship* (Word Publishing, 1988), Ch. 5, 'Praise and Worship'.
[2] *op.cit.*, p.44.
[3] See *Worship* (Kingsway, 1987), Ch. 12, 'Leading Worship 1'.
[4] *op.cit.*, p.147.

In each of these three accounts the ultimate aim of worship is seen as the intimate encounter with God. One of the characteristics of the Charismatic Movement is that it has restored this sense of the importance of the face-to-face relationship between the individual and God in Christ, not only in the context of private individual worship but also in public worship.

This mode of worship is used as a framework for leading 'open worship' in charismatic churches, and the celebration style meetings appear to be structured on this basis.[1] However the question needs to be asked as to how appropriate it is to structure a corporate event around what is predominantly an individual experience.[1] Phil Rogers in fact does not consider this mode of worship to be a model for corporate worship precisely because it describes an experience. This emphasis on intimacy also raises the question of what should be the nature and content of corporate intimacy with God within worship. The most obvious examples of corporate intimacy in the New Testament are the descriptions of meals, particularly common in Luke's writing. In Luke's Gospel one of the main themes of these meals is Jesus welcoming sinners by eating with them, culminating of course with the Last Supper. This Biblical material points to Communion as being the most appropriate setting for corporate intimacy, Jesus reclining at table amongst sinners.

4. A Response

Restorationists consider it strange that Anglicans should want to continue with a liturgical text. This is not so much because they are against structure, but because in their approach to restructuring their own worship they have tended to take pride in the fact that they have been able to throw out the old and start afresh with Biblical patterns of worship. The reason, however, why Anglicans persist with their liturgical texts is not simply because they are obliged by Canon Law so to do, but because they believe that such texts provide Biblical expression to the nature of God's worshipping people. From within this context a number of comments can be made about Restorationist worship.

(i) There is a tendency for worship to be synonymous with the music and song part of a worship event. For example, David Fellingham's chapter on 'The History of the Worshipping Church' in *Worship Restored* appears to concentrate on the history of psalms, hymns and spiritual songs in Christian worship.[2] This emphasis within Restorationism is no doubt due to the fact that those who write in detail about worship are themselves musicians. The assumption that worship is primarily to do with worship and song is not confined to Restorationism, but seems to receive widespread acceptance. It surfaces, for example, when a church calls their group of musicians 'the worship group'. Technically speaking, of course, the congregation is 'the worship group'! The problem with this line of thinking is that it downgrades other legitimate expressions of worship. Anglican liturgy attempts to incorporate the variety of modes of worship found in Scripture. This means not only singing and music, but also listen-

---

[1] See D. Fellingham, *Worship Restored*, p.114.
[2] Those who write above would regard this experience as being corporate as well as individual. 16.

ing and attending to God's word through Scripture reading and preaching (cf. Psalm 119 and 1 Timothy 4.13), intercession (cf. 1 Timothy 2.1-2) and communion (cf. 1 Corinthians 11.23-26). These three modes of worship provide the structure for the ASB Communion service.

(ii) Restorationist worship lacks much of the objectivity which is so much part of Anglican liturgical worship. One of the reasons for this is because Restorationists want to be flexible in their worship, and don't want to be tied to a set structure. Another important contributory factor is that revelation from God is often portrayed as a subjective experience of God making Himself real to me now. Externals are seen to be subsidiary to the primary emphasis of worship being a matter of the heart. To an Anglican who is used to the objectivity of a liturgy focused on Word and Sacrament this is unsatisfactory. Nick de Keyser, a charismatic Anglo-Catholic, comments that liturgy 'centres us on God, liberates from subjectiveness and self-centredness, and safeguards us from the whims of individual leaders'.[2] The presence of a corporate confession of faith, for example, enables the church to recognize that which is properly Christian about the faith and practice, and stands over against any misguided beliefs.

(iii) Restorationists rightly emphasize the important role the individual has in contributing to corporate worship. There remains the question of whether their worship is an adequate corporate expression of the life of God's people. This is not to say that they do not recognize the importance of the church as a body, with each member belonging to the others. However, with such a stress on individual participation within worship one asks whether enough emphasis is given to the corporate expression of worship. Again, one of the main aims of a liturgical structure is to facilitate this corporate expression.

¹ *Worship Restored*, Ch. 2—let the reader decide!
² Anglican Renewal Ministries Magazine *(Armlink)*, No. 38, (Autumn 1989), p.13.

4. FACING THE CHALLENGE

It is in the nature of the radical Christianity practised by Restorationists that it challenges those outside the movement to re-evaluate their response to the Gospel. This is no less the case with the Restorationist claim that God is restoring true worship to the church in their midst. This last section will indicate areas in which Anglicans could learn from their worship.

Music and Worship

One of the most important emphases in Restoration worship is the creative use of music and song. Such creativity is by no means confined to Restorationism[1], but nevertheless it provides a number of important insights:

(a) The importance of using the musical gifts of the congregation. Those churches who rely simply upon organ or piano accompaniment could profitably consider how they could expand their accompaniment to include other musical instruments. The working model for such accompaniment offered by the Restorationists is the music group in which there would be a variety of instruments with some singers and a worship leader. Some Anglican churches already make use of this style of music group to assist in leading worship. Within a liturgical setting such groups can be used in a variety of ways. For example, in Morning Prayer or Family Service a group could be used as a response to confession and absolution, or in response to the readings from Scripture. In Communion the administration is often a time when groups are used. If churches are seeking to develop this kind of music group then training conferences are organized by the Christian Music Association (C.M.A.).[2]

(b) The importance of using music to engage the worshipper's being. One of the characteristics of the style of music in Restoration circles is its accessibility to the majority of contemporary worshippers. In common with much of the renewal music, the style is middle-of-the-road (a Radio 2 feel!), and easy to engage with. But the use of music goes beyond this, as is clear from David Fellingham's suggestion of using instruments to interpret God's character or message. Within a liturgical structure, an instrument or instruments could be used in this way as a response to the reading from the Scriptures, focussing on an aspect of the reading, and thereby drawing the congregation into the spoken Word.

(c) The importance of musicians having a Christian commitment to serve their congregation. The Restorationist leaders appoint musicians not only on the basis of musical ability but also on the understanding that they will have the Christian maturity to work with those in leadership to serve the worshipping community. The difficulties that arise from a choir or organist who have little Christian conviction should be enough to convince any Anglican that the Restorationists are on the right track.

[1] See Andrew Maries *One Heart, One Voice* (Hodder and Stoughton, 1986) for an example of recent charismatic Anglican writing on music and worship.
[2] C.M.A., Glyndley Manor, Stone Cross, Eastbourne, East Sussex, BN24 5BS. 18.

(d) The importance of making hymnody accessible to the worshipper. The often simple structure, focussed truth and musical style of many Restoration songs makes it easy for the contemporary worshipper to grasp hold of and linger on a Biblical truth. Indeed the verdict of the newly converted Christian who has had little or no experience of traditional hymnody is often to find this contemporary style of hymnody far more accessible. This presents a dilemma for Anglicans who may want to encourage the use of the new songs but also want to maintain the traditional hymnody with its important doctrinal emphases. One answer to this dilemma would be to settle upon a repertoire of traditional hymns (maybe 80-90), and then through education and use help the congregation to see the lasting value of these hymns.

Form, Flow and Spontaneity

Restorationism has always been highly suspicious of using liturgical texts in worship, and for a variety of reasons. First, these texts are often seen as a sell-out to legalism, akin to the religious ceremonies Paul condemns (Galatians 4.9-11; Colossians 2.16-23). Phil Rogers, quoting these passages, writes:

'We are not under a covenant of law with rules and regulations laid down, but under a covenant of grace that operates by the direct leading of the Holy Spirit. Now some would argue that the liturgies that the Church has developed over generations are the result of the Spirit's leading. But such liturgies are by their nature legalistic; some are even upheld by ecclesiastical law. The Holy Spirit never leads us into legalism.'[1]

Bound up with this charge of legalism is a suspicion of religious externals. These are often viewed as a barrier to the worshipper being open to the Spirit of God. Secondly, the influence of the independent roots of the majority of Restoration churches would militate against any liturgical pattern being adopted 'from the outside'.

However, alongside this rejection of any set liturgical text, there is a recognition that it is important to have form and order in worship. This form for a worship meeting is provided by the worship leader, who will have prepared a structure beforehand.[1] David Fellingham in writing of the importance of this preparation by leaders argues the point by acknowledging structure in the Psalms:

'If the worship leader has a sense of form and order as a guideline, it will help him feel secure in his leadership. This is also Biblical as the Psalms have form and structure. As the worship leader prepares there is no reason why the form and structure cannot be invaded by the Holy Spirit.'[1]

[1] It is interesting to note that in Restorationist accounts of the Tabernacle of David, worship at Jerusalem is seen as prefiguring the era of grace. This is contrasted with the sacrificial system at Gibeon, which is seen as an old way of worship under law. See, e.g., *Creative Worship*, pp.41, 43, and *Worship Restored*, pp.41-49.
[2] *Learning to Worship*, p.72. 19.
[3] This is more so in the case of a celebration.
[4] *Worship Restored*, p.115.

This recognition of the importance of form has no doubt grown out of the experience of worship leaders. New Life Christian Fellowship, for example, write of the importance of pre-planning by worship leaders and musicians: 'Some people may object to discussing beforehand. They feel this can take the spontaneity out of the meeting. They say, "Why don't you just let it happen?" We have tried that method and prefer discussion'.[1]

An example of a typical song structure for a celebration[2] would be to begin with songs concentrating on praise and thanksgiving (e.g. I will enter his gates with thanksgiving in my heart (252 SHF), God of glory, we exalt your name (136 SHF)), then move to quieter, more meditative songs (e.g. Jesus, you are the radiance of the Father's glory (298 SHF)), and finish with a sense of proclamation and going out (e.g. For this purpose Christ was revealed (110 SHF)). The level of song preparation by the worship leader in a congregational meeting would be much less since the congregation would have the opportunity to contribute songs.

Within this form however, the leader has to be sensitive to the Holy Spirit's leading, and thus must have a sense of the flow of the meeting. 'Flow' is an important concept for Restorationist. It is used to describe worship which goes on without unnecessary interruptions (e.g. the worship leader saying too much), and which carries everyone in the same direction. It is also a way of describing the Spirit's leading of a meeting. David Fellingham, in writing of the need for worship leaders to be sensitive to the flow, compares the worship leader to a bird of prey who rides 'the thermals of the Holy Spirit'.[3] To enhance flow leaders are advised to make preparation a priority and close working relationships are encouraged. New Life Christian Fellowship have discovered familiarity and unity between worship leaders and musicians[4] is essential to good flow. Chris Bowater widens the application of this to encompass unity within the congregation, drawing upon Psalm 133. 'It is when hearts are united, one in love and one in purpose, not merely in words, that truly it can be said, "We flow together".'[5]

It is in the light of an appreciation of form and flow that spontaneity (another of the hallmarks of Restorationist worship) is to be understood. The Pocket Oxford Dictionary's definition of 'spontaneous' is as follows: 'Resulting from natural impulse, nor forced or suggested or caused from outside, instructive or automatic, volunteered or unconstrained, not deliberate or laboured'. In other words, spontaneity is a creative step arising from the flow of a meeting, rather than an interruption of flow. This understanding of spontaneity is implicit in much of what is written by Restorationists on the form and flow meetings. For example, Chris Bowater writes. 'You can only be truly flexible when you are truly fully prepared'.[6] It is also emphasized that if there are any contributions by worshippers they must be within the flow of the meeting. It seems therefore that Restorationists are working (implicitly rather than explicitly) with a synthesis of form, flow and spontaneity.

[1] Ten Worshipping Churches, p.98.
[2] See Worship Restored, pp.114, 115.
[3] Worship Restored, p.108.
[4] Ten Worshipping Churches, p.99.
[5] Creative Worship, p.12.
[6] Creative Worship, p.134.

Anglicans are of course used to the concept of form in worship. The phenomenon of a liturgical text is not simply an acknowledgement of the importance of form in worship, but also a way of giving visible context and shape to the nature of God's people as they worship. The Restorationist emphasis on flow is interesting. Chris Walsh refers to the concept of flow as elaborated by Mihali Csikszemtmihalyi:

'"Flow" is for him a state in which action follows action according to an internal logic which seems to need no conscious intervention on our part; we experience it as a unified flowing from one moment to the next, in which we feel in control of our actions, and in which there is little distinction between self and environment, between stimulus and response, or between past, present and future. He sees flow as a common experience whenever people act with total involvement ...'[1]

One of the criticisms often made by charismatics is that the liturgy does not flow. Taking note of the Restorationists' experience of the need for preparation and good relationships to enhance flow and spontaneity, one of the implications this would have for liturgical worship would be to ensure that the congregation is in relationship to the liturgy. There is a need for congregations to 'own' their liturgy so that its dynamics and content ('the internal logic') become familiar enough to facilitate flow and spontaneity. This points to churches making liturgical worship a high priority focus for their teaching programme (e.g. confirmation groups, housegroups, or an adult education programme).

Accessibility of Worship
One of the reasons that there is often a flow to Restorationist worship is because of its accessibility to the contemporary worshipper (although those worshippers with a more traditional understanding of worship would probably not be able to enter into it so easily). The worship is designed to be culturally relevant to the ordinary 'man in the street', an emphasis which arises from the evangelistic thrust of the Movement. This is reflected in a variety of ways. use of music and song (which has already been discussed), the emphasis on informality, the familiarity of many of the buildings used, few books, and appropriate cultural expressions of worship. One interesting example of this is the phenomenon of clapping after a rousing praise song. To many Anglicans the idea of 'giving God a clap' would indicate shallowness in worship. In everyday life, however, clapping is often reserved for the truly outstanding and worthy of praise, and therefore may not be out of place as a means of expressing appreciation for God's goodness.

The challenge for Anglican worship is for it to be related to the culture it is intended to serve. For example, in areas where books are rare, or alternatively on a shelf but rarely used, it is culturally insensitive to be handing out a pile of books to those who venture into church on a Sunday. We also

[1] Chris Walsh in *Symbolism and the Liturgy I* (Grove Liturgical Studies, no.23, 1980), p.23.

live in a highly visual society, a fact which emphasises the opportunity of having liturgical texts accompanied by illustrations, indicating the activity appropriate in the various stages of the liturgy. Such illustrations could be either prepared for O.H.P. use, or printed with a service order. In order for a congregation to 'own' a liturgy, attempts have to be made to enable them to feel that it is 'their' liturgy.

The Worshipper as Participant—Prophets, Priests and Kings

Complementary to the accessibilty of Restorationist worship is the fact that the worshippers are expected to participate fully in the worship event. This is particularly the case with the congregation and cell style meetings, where every member contribution is encouraged. How in practice could Anglican liturgical worship be said to enable participation? On one level, particularly if one views participation in a corporate sense, it can be said to be total, in that the liturgy is designed to facilitate participation by the whole congregation, whether it be together or at points led by individuals. On another level however, especially when individual contributions are given a high value, the liturgy is seen as restrictive. Anglican churches, seeking to respond positively to this latter view, tend either to let services, or parts of services, go 'free', or make available settings outside the Sunday worship where this kind of participation can take place (e.g. housegroups or a mid-week meeting). However the problem with such discussion on levels of participation is that it easily gets lost in definitions of 'participation', and can fail to focus adequately on the underlying theological categories describing the worshipping Church. In this respect, the emphasis given by David Fellingham on the Calvinist perspective of redeemed mankind as prophet, priest and king is of greater challenge than discussing levels of participation. In a culture which tends to assume that human beings are closed to the transcendent (definition of human beings is often only in scientific, technological or economic terms), it is of importance that the Church seeks to recover a theological anthropology. Exploring the nature of Christians as prophets, priests and kings would be a way of doing this, and thus of gaining a richer theological perspective of the worshipper, or the worshipping Church, as participant. This can be illustrated by the way Restorationists regard all worshippers as priests.

The theological basis of this emphasis lies in the priestly nature of the worshipper (e.g. 'you are a royal priesthood', 1 Peter 2.9). There is a strong sense that because of Christ's atoning death Christians are set free to offer worship (in the form of praise and prayer). Phil Rogers writes of an individual participating:

'As a priest to the Lord Most High, we may be called upon at any time to step out from the congregation of priests gathered before the throne of his holiness and majesty to offer our sacrifice of prayer and praise to the Lord of Glory. As we step forward, our Advocate stands beside us, holding our hands. As the Father sees him, so he accepts us'.[1]

One of the marks of the use of the Tabernacle of David model is that it provides a model for bringing praise to God; it is a 'from us to God' movement. David's dancing before the Lord with all his might with his linen ephod prefigures the wholehearted giving of praise by the Christian worshipper. The wholehearted bodily expression of Restorationism is an expression of

[1] *Learning to Worship* (1988), p.85.

this priestly ministry. This ministry is also reflected in songs which speak of 'lifting up holy hands' (e.g. 581 SHF), or of praise being likened to incense (e.g. 313 SHF).

Worshippers are seen then, not only as ministers of the Lord, but also as ministers *to* the Lord. Such an emphasis is a direct challenge to the way of thinking that views worshippers in a passive or receptive mode. The introductory sentence to Morning and Evening Prayer makes it clear that Christians gather in worship in God's presence 'to offer him praise and thanksgiving, to hear and receive his holy word.' Evangelicals, in being inherently suspicious of the terminology of offering with its Catholic overtones and at home with the proclamation of the Word, have a tendency to downgrade the offering of praise. Worshippers are thus cast in a more receptive and passive mode. Perhaps this is one reason why some Anglicans are reluctant to use their bodies in worship. The Restoration emphasis is a challenge to recover a proper sense of the worshipper as one who offers praise. Rowan Williams, an Anglo-Catholic Anglican, writes: 'The effect of Christ's sacrifice is precisely to make us "liturgical" beings, capable of offering ourselves, our praises and our symbolic gifts to a God who we know will receive us in Christ'.[1]

God in the Midst
'Jesus, we enthrone You,
We proclaim You our King,
Standing here in the midst of us
We raise You up with our praise.
And as we worship build a throne,
And as we worship build a throne,
And as we worship build a throne,
Come Lord Jesus and take your place.'[2]

It has already been emphasized that worship for Restorationists is primarily a matter of knowing God in their midst. Along with other charismatics they expect worship to be an experience of the Spirit of God amongst them, transforming their lives. However, Restorationists would also want to go further and say that worship is the specific context in which God is experienced or most totally present. Psalm 22.3 is often quoted in this connection, a verse which speaks of God being enthroned on the praises of Israel. The above song is based on this verse and illustrates the way in which worship creates an environment in which God's presence can be realised. Some might regard such language as 'enthroning Jesus', and 'raising Jesus up' as inappropriate (since Jesus is already exalted), but the fundamental insight of the song is the same as that expressed by James 4.8. 'Draw near to God and he will draw near to you'.

The notion that praise and worship can create space for God to reveal himself is taken up by a recent study on the nature of praise by Daniel

[1] Rowan Williams, *Eucharistic Sacrifice—The Roots of a Metaphor* (Grove Liturgical Study No.31, 1982), p.27.
[2] SHF 343.